Connections!

ART

CAROLINE GRIMSHAW

ART CONSULTANTS

ANDREA FINN

JULIA WEINER EDUCATION OFFICER

AT THE COURTAULD INSTITUTE GALLERIES, LONDON

WORLD BOOK
In association with
TWO-CAN

Connections!

ART

CREATIVE AND EDITORIAL DIRECTOR
CONCEPT/FORMAT/DESIGN/TEXT
CAROLINE GRIMSHAW

ART CONSULTANTS
ANDREA FINN
JULIA WEINER EDUCATION OFFICER
AT THE COURTAULD INSTITUTE GALLERIES, LONDON

ILLUSTRATIONS
NICK DUFFY ☆ **SPIKE GERRELL** ☆ **JO MOORE**

THANKS TO
LYNDSEY PRICE PICTURE RESEARCH
CLAIRE YUDE AND **BRONWEN LEWIS** EDITORIAL SUPPORT
IQBAL HUSSAIN TEXT
AND **CHARLES SHAAR MURRAY**
TIM SANPHER ☆ **ANDREW JARVIS**

TITLES IN THIS SERIES →
☆ PEOPLE
☆ BUILDINGS
☆ EARTH
☆ ART
☆ MUSIC

FIRST PUBLISHED IN THE UNITED STATES IN 1996 BY
WORLD BOOK, INC.
525 W. MONROE
20TH FLOOR
CHICAGO, IL USA 60661
IN ASSOCIATION WITH TWO-CAN PUBLISHING LTD.

COPYRIGHT © CAROLINE GRIMSHAW 1996

FOR INFORMATION ON OTHER WORLD BOOK PRODUCTS,
CALL 1-800-255-1750, X 2238.

ISBN: 0-7166-1758-7 (PBK.) ISBN: 0-7166-1757-9 (HBK.)
LC: 96-60456

PRINTED IN HONG KONG
1 2 3 4 5 6 7 8 9 10 99 98 97 96

2

Contents

PART → PAGE 3

1 LET'S TAKE A LOOK AT
ART

PART → PAGE 11

2 IT'S TIME TO THINK ABOUT
MAKING ART

PART → PAGE 23

3 ART MAKES AN
IMPACT!

**DISCOVER THE CONNECTIONS THROUGH
QUESTIONS AND ANSWERS...**
YOU CAN READ THIS BOOK FROM START TO FINISH OR
LEAP-FROG THROUGH THE SECTIONS
FOLLOWING THE PATHS SUGGESTED
IN THESE SPECIAL "CONNECT! BOXES." **Connect!**

**ENJOY YOUR JOURNEY OF
DISCOVERY AND UNDERSTANDING**

Let's take a look at

art

What is it and who makes it?

Who made the first art?

Why does the world need art?

Can art be made by a machine?

You'll find all these questions (and more!)
answered in PART ONE of your journey of discovery
and understanding. Turn the page! --->

QUESTION 1 What is art?

Art is a collection of ideas produced by human skill, imagination and invention.

Artists share their ideas by making or selecting pictures, sounds and words to create an art form.

THIS MAY BE VISUAL (SUCH AS PAINTING, DRAWING, SCULPTURE AND DANCE).

IT MAY BE SOMETHING THAT YOU CAN HEAR (SUCH AS MUSIC).

IT MAY BE SOMETHING YOU READ (SUCH AS A STORY OR A POEM).

Sometimes it is a combination of more than one of these things.

This book takes you on a journey of exploration of the VISUAL ARTS. In Western cultures, two of the main types of visual art are painting and sculpture. Other countries have their own traditions. For example, Islamic visual arts concentrate on decoration. Objects and buildings are decorated with complex geometric patterns and fine handwriting called calligraphy. Other cultures specialize in masks, pottery, metalwork, and even body decoration, such as tattoos.

⬆ A highly-patterned mosque in Iran.

☆ THE VISUAL ARTS INCLUDE ANY WAY OF MAKING AN IMAGE OR OBJECT THAT CAN BE SEEN OR VISUALIZED.

Connect!

CAN ART BE MADE BY A MACHINE? SEE Q13.

Prove It!

Only one of these pictures shows a work of art. Can you guess which one it is? The answer is hidden on page 5.

1

2

3

QUESTION 2 Who makes art? (AND WHY DO THEY BOTHER?)

Some things are made by people to serve practical needs, such as tools for digging or eating. Other objects are made because they are interesting or instructive to look at. An artist is someone who is involved in this kind of creation.

People make art...

TO EARN A LIVING.   TO TELL THE WORLD WHAT THEY THINK.

TO SHOW WHAT THEY, OR OTHER PEOPLE, BELIEVE IN.

TO ENTERTAIN OR STIMULATE THEMSELVES AND OTHER PEOPLE.

TO EXPLORE NEW WAYS OF LOOKING AT FAMILIAR OBJECTS AND SCENES.

Connect!

SOME ARTISTS FEEL THEY NEED TO MAKE ART TO SURVIVE. IT IS THEIR "CALLING" OR MISSION. SEE Q36.

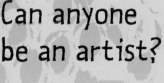

QUESTION 3

Can anyone be an artist?

Connect!

SOME ARTISTS HAVE BEEN FASCINATED BY ART MADE BY CHILDREN. SEE Q34.

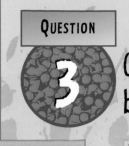

Yes! One of the first creative things a child does is pick up a crayon or pen and scribble.

☆ "NAIVE" ARTISTS

Artists who have not been trained are sometimes called "naive." They may know little about the history of art, or its rules. They make art that is often simple, fresh, and almost innocent.

CASE STUDY

NAME: **HENRI ROUSSEAU** (1844–1910)

NATIONALITY: French

At the age of 41, this "self-taught" artist left his job at the Paris Customs Office to spend more time on his art. His brightly-colored jungle paintings were admired by the Spanish painter **PABLO PICASSO** (1881–1973). Picasso owned several of Rousseau's paintings and in 1908 held a famous party in his honor.

Connect!

PICASSO IS PERHAPS THE MOST FAMOUS ARTIST OF THE TWENTIETH CENTURY. LEARN MORE ABOUT HIM IN Q43.

← *The Beach at Trouville* (1870), by **CLAUDE MONET** (1840–1926).

QUESTION 4

Who made the first art?

There is evidence from all over the world that our prehistoric ancestors were artists. The earliest examples were made between 40,000 and 10,000 BC.

☆ FROM CHIPPING STONES TO MAKING ART...

2 MILLION YEARS AGO	in east central Africa—Homo habilis made tools from pebbles.
1 MILLION YEARS AGO	in Africa—Homo erectus made cutting edges by chipping away at stones.
1 MILLION YEARS AGO	in China—Homo erectus learned to use fire.
125,000 YEARS AGO	in Europe and west Asia—Neanderthal man made a variety of tools and painted his body with red ochre (a type of soil).
42,000 YEARS AGO	in Asia and Europe—Homo sapiens carved the first works of art.

⬆ The Lascaux cave paintings in France were discovered in 1940 by a group of schoolboys. The bulls, horses and deer were painted around 17,000 years ago.

☆ CAVE PAINTINGS...

The best examples of prehistoric art are found in the caves of south-western France and northern Spain, as well as in South Africa and Australia. The hunting peoples of Europe were inspired by the animals around them, which is why they often painted herds of cattle, deer, horses, bison and even mammoths.

HOW WERE THEY PAINTED?

● Early colors were made from burned wood and bones, chalk, soils and powdered minerals, mixed with either water or animal fat.

● The picture outlines were painted with fingers, moss, or brushes made from chewed twigs, fur or feathers. One way of filling in the outlines was by spraying powder through tubes made of bone.

Prove It!

Look closely at this painting. It shows us how people dressed and relaxed 125 years ago. To find out what else the artist was trying to tell us, ask yourself these questions:

1. HOW DOES THE PAINTING MAKE YOU FEEL?

2. WHAT DOES THE PAINTING REMIND YOU OF?

3. HAVE YOU EVER SEEN SAND AND SKY LOOK LIKE THIS?

Connect!

TURN TO Q25 TO SEE HOW ARTISTS USE COLOR TO MOVE US. IN Q26 FIND OUT HOW THE IMPRESSIONISTS USED COLOR TO PAINT LIGHT.

☆ **PROVE IT!** ANSWER: PICTURE **2** IS A WORK OF ART—IT IS PART OF A SCULPTURE BY **CARL ANDRE** (BORN IN 1932) CALLED *EQUIVALENT VIII*; PICTURE **1** IS A BRICK WALL; PICTURE **3** IS A PIECE OF DECORATIVE WRAPPING PAPER.

QUESTION 5

Does art have to be flat?

Not at all. Artists can choose to make art out of any materials they like. Art can be three-dimensional.

Humans have been making and carving figures for thousands of years, using stone, metal, wood and ivory, as well as the horns and teeth of animals, feathers, shells and dried grasses.

☆ WHAT IS SCULPTURE?

Sculpture is the name given to art that is three-dimensional. Most sculptures are freestanding, which means they can be walked around and viewed from any angle. However, bas-relief sculptures are carved out of a flat surface so that the pictures are raised and stand out from the background.

Connect! ART IS EVERYWHERE—ON CEILINGS, FLOORS AND WALLS. SEE Q28.

☆ EXAMINE THESE EXAMPLES OF SCULPTURE

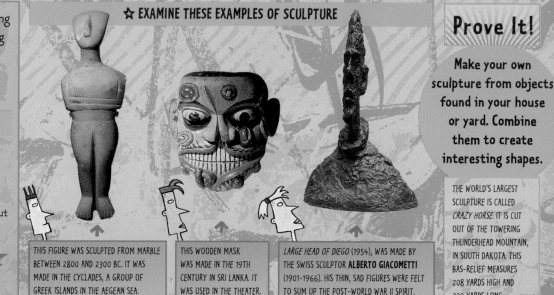

THIS FIGURE WAS SCULPTED FROM MARBLE BETWEEN 2800 AND 2300 BC. IT WAS MADE IN THE CYCLADES, A GROUP OF GREEK ISLANDS IN THE AEGEAN SEA.

THIS WOODEN MASK WAS MADE IN THE 19TH CENTURY IN SRI LANKA. IT WAS USED IN THE THEATER.

LARGE HEAD OF DIEGO (1954), WAS MADE BY THE SWISS SCULPTOR **ALBERTO GIACOMETTI** (1901-1966). HIS THIN, SAD FIGURES WERE FELT TO SUM UP THE POST-WORLD WAR II SPIRIT.

Prove It!

Make your own sculpture from objects found in your house or yard. Combine them to create interesting shapes.

THE WORLD'S LARGEST SCULPTURE IS CALLED *CRAZY HORSE.* IT IS CUT OUT OF THE TOWERING THUNDERHEAD MOUNTAIN, IN SOUTH DAKOTA. THIS BAS-RELIEF MEASURES 208 YARDS HIGH AND 230 YARDS LONG.

Connect! WHAT STRANGE MATERIALS DO ARTISTS USE? FIND OUT IN Q16 AND Q27.

QUESTION 6

Why does the world need art?

Why we make art, and what we use it for, is called its function. Here are some examples of art's function...

1 ART IS MADE TO DECORATE OUR WORLD.

2 ART TELLS US ABOUT OUR WORLD.

3 ART DESCRIBES AND EXPLAINS OUR HISTORY.

4 ART IS USED TO HELP HEAL THE SICK.

5 ART HELPS US TO EXPLORE OUR WORLD.

Some art is made to frighten viewers, or even amaze them. In Africa and Sri Lanka, art plays an important part in rituals and everyday life. Masks are often worn just once before being abandoned.

Connect! SOME ART IS CREATED BY PEOPLE WITH STRANGE IMAGINATIONS AND TORTURED SOULS. CHECK OUT Q37.

☆ ART CAN BE PART OF EVERYDAY LIFE

People from every culture make art. In some cultures art is more connected to everyday life than in others. Art used to be present in nearly all aspects of the lives of the native peoples of North America.

THE IROQUOIS TRIBE MADE WOODEN MASKS, WHICH THEY BELIEVED COULD CURE ILLNESSES. WOODLAND TRIBES DECORATED THEIR BODIES WITH PAINTS. THE TRIBES ON THE NORTHWEST COAST CARVED BRIGHTLY COLORED POSTS OUT OF ENTIRE TREE TRUNKS UP TO 89 FEET HIGH. THESE TOTEM POLES WERE ERECTED OUTSIDE PEOPLE'S HOMES AND RECORDED THE HISTORY OF THE FAMILIES LIVING INSIDE.

Connect! SOME ARTISTS HAVE TRIED TO BRING MANY PEOPLE INTO CONTACT WITH THEIR IDEAS AND WORK. SEE Q49.

7

When did we start framing paintings and hanging them in special places, such as galleries?

In the past, artists have presented their work in many ways and for many reasons. Galleries are quite a new idea.

● The Paleolithic artists, working between around 20,000 and 8,000 BC, used the rough walls of the cave to paint on. The cave artists set no boundaries for their paintings and had no idea about the use of background or frames. The paintings showed what was crucial to them – hunting animals for food.

● In ancient Egypt, artists painted large scenes on the plaster walls of houses and temples. The best preserved paintings were found in the burial chambers of the wealthy, painted on the tomb walls, and often "boxed-in" on panels. Symbols called hieroglyphs decorated the background.

● During the 15th and 16th centuries, artists in the West began to experiment with new techniques to make their work look more realistic, such as painting light and shade and using perspective. Artists made art for palaces and public places, and for the walls and ceilings of churches.

● The easel picture was a medium-sized painting that was made at the artist's easel. They were portable, and could be framed and used to decorate a house, or hung in galleries. Because many more people could buy these paintings, by the 17th century there was a larger range of subject matter, including paintings of landscapes, farms, houses, boats, everyday life, work and leisure.

Connect! MANY ARTISTS HAVE USED ANIMALS IN THEIR WORK. SEE Q29 AND Q30.

Connect! GALLERIES ARE A PLACE WHERE PEOPLE CAN SEE ART. HOW ELSE ARE IDEAS SHARED? SEE Q41.

THE ARTIST PICASSO ONCE SAID: "A PAINTING IS 'DONE FOR' AS SOON AS IT IS BOUGHT AND HUNG ON A WALL." HE WAS AFRAID THAT THE PAINTING WOULD BECOME LIKE WALLPAPER!

⬆ *The Marriage Contract* (1743), by **WILLIAM HOGARTH** (1697-1764).

8 Should art be permanent?

Not all art is made to last forever. Some is deliberately created to have a limited lifespan.

Prove It!

EGYPTIAN SCULPTURE WAS MADE FROM PRECIOUS METALS, BRONZE AND HARD STONES. THIS WORK WAS INTENDED TO LAST FOREVER, REFLECTING THE IMPORTANCE OF THE PIECE OF ART AND THE SUBJECT.

MARBLE STATUES MADE BY THE ROMANS WERE INTENDED TO LAST FOREVER. THE ARTIST AND THE PERSON WHO COMMISSIONED THE WORK WANTED TO SUGGEST THAT THE PEOPLE PORTRAYED WERE NOT JUST POWERFUL BUT IMMORTAL TOO.

THE ARTIST **ANYA GALLACCIO** (BORN IN 1963) USES FLOWERS IN HER WORK. IN *HEAD OVER HEELS* (1995) THEY ARE SUSPENDED IN SPACE AND GRADUALLY DIE. THIS PROCESS OF DECAY IS PART OF THE ARTIST'S MESSAGE.

Make a face sculpture using items of food as your materials. Lay everything out on a background of lettuce leaves. This art is not permanent, but it is edible!

Connect! WHAT IS CONSERVATION? SEE Q46.

Connect! CAN ART BE AN EVENT? FIND OUT IN Q44.

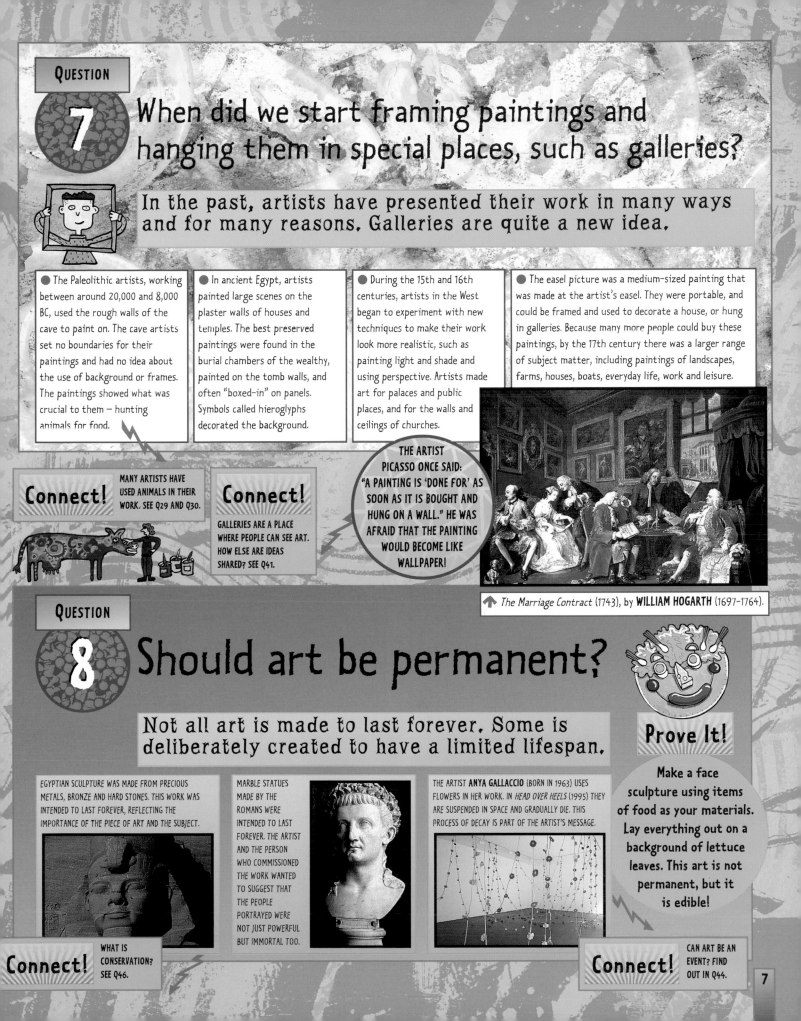

QUESTION

9 How do we make sense of art?

What we see when we look at art depends on our experience and knowledge, our mood and imagination and what the artist wants to show us.

WE USE OUR SENSES TO APPRECIATE ART

☆ THE ARTIST   ☆ THE WORK   ☆ YOU, THE VIEWER

THE ARTIST MAY HAVE A MESSAGE

THE ARTIST MAKES DECISIONS

ASK YOURSELF: HAVE YOU SEEN SOMETHING LIKE THIS BEFORE?

ASK YOURSELF:
WHAT IS THE SUBJECT? WHAT MATERIALS ARE USED? IS THERE A TITLE? WHEN AND WHERE WAS IT MADE? HOW BIG IS IT? WHAT COLOR IS IT? DO YOU LIKE IT? HOW DOES IT MAKE YOU FEEL?

SIGHT WE SEE THE COLOR, SIZE, SHAPE AND MATERIALS USED.
TOUCH WE CAN SOMETIMES FEEL THE TEXTURE OF THE MATERIALS CHOSEN BY THE ARTIST, SUCH AS STONE, METAL OR CANVAS.
SMELL SOME ARTISTS USE MATERIALS SUCH AS FLOWERS AND CHOCOLATE BECAUSE OF THEIR DISTINCTIVE SMELLS.
HEARING ARTISTS MAY COMBINE PICTURES WITH SOUND.

↑ *Merry-Go-Round* (1916), by **MARK GERTLER** (1891–1939).

1 WHAT ARE THE PEOPLE IN THE PAINTING WEARING?

2 DO THEY LOOK AS IF THEY ARE HAVING A GOOD TIME?

3 HOW DO YOU FEEL WHEN YOU LOOK AT THIS IMAGE – HAPPY OR UNEASY?

The figures in the painting are actually in uniform and look as if they are screaming. The top of the merry-go-round looks like a rocket. The artist was using the painting to express the horror he felt for World War I (1914–18).

Connect!

TURN TO Q18 TO FIND OUT WHAT KIND OF DECISIONS AN ARTIST MUST MAKE.

Prove It!

At first glance, this painting looks bright and its title sounds happy. Now, examine it more closely and then answer the questions.

QUESTION

10 Can you appreciate art if you can't see it?

Connect!

WHAT DOES ART TELL US ABOUT HISTORY? CHECK OUT Q38.

Yes, art can be experienced and enjoyed by people who are partially-sighted or even completely blind.

People may suffer from eye defects and diseases, which sometimes cause blindness. Some people see nothing at all. Others see light but nothing else. Blind and partially-sighted people may have once been able to see, so they may use their memories to help them to appreciate art.

● Blind people can explore art by touching the surface of a painting or sculpture. They can feel the texture and temperature of the material and the shape of the work.

● Special three-dimensional diagrams called "thermoforms" are made of paintings. A blind person can use these to actually feel what is going on in the work of art.

● Tape cassettes and books written in raised lettering called braille give information about art. Some galleries also have signs and labels translated into braille.

Connect!

WHO MADE ONE OF THE FIRST ABSTRACT PAINTINGS? CHECK OUT Q34.

QUESTION 11 What is abstract art?

A painting, image or sculpture that uses shapes, colors and patterns—rather than showing objects, scenes and people as they appear to look in real life—may be called "abstract" art.

Art may become more about the artist's moods, feelings and opinions, expressed through color and form, rather than the appearance of real things.

ASK YOURSELF:
● HOW DID THE ARTIST FEEL MAKING IT?
● WHY DID THE ARTIST MAKE THIS PAINTING?
● HOW DO I FEEL LOOKING AT IT?

1953 BY **CLYFFORD STILL** REMINDS SOME PEOPLE OF THE COUNTRYSIDE IN THE AMERICAN WEST. THE ARTIST FELT THAT THE EARTH'S LANDSCAPES ARE LIKE THE HUMAN IMAGINATION—THEY HAVE NO LIMITS.

⬆ *1953* (1953), by **CLYFFORD STILL** (1904-80).

QUESTION 12 Can art be an idea?

Yes.

Art is like a language. Artists use their work to communicate messages and ideas. In the late 1960s some artists thought that the content of their art was the thought processes and ideas that went into making it. They called this "conceptual" art.

☆ IT MAKES YOU THINK...

IN 1965 THE AMERICAN ARTIST **JOSEPH KOSUTH** MADE A WORK OF ART CALLED *CLOCK*. THIS WAS MADE UP OF A REAL CLOCK, A PHOTOGRAPH OF THAT CLOCK AND SOME WORDS TAKEN FROM A DICTIONARY EXPLAINING WHAT TIME, MACHINES AND OBJECTS ARE.

Connect! HOW DID ONE FAMOUS ARTIST STOP HIS WORK FROM BECOMING TOO ABSTRACT? SEE Q16.

QUESTION 13 Can art be made by a machine?

Yes, some artists use machines to make art. Others have been inspired by machines, speed and power.

☆ THE FUTURISTS

A group of artists calling themselves the Futurists declared in 1909 that artists should create art that showed the speed, movement and machinery of the new century.

☆ THE VORTICISTS

A group called the Vorticists was formed in 1913 by the English writer and artist **WYNDHAM LEWIS** (1884-1957). One Vorticist, **JACOB EPSTEIN** (1880-1959), was so excited by mechanical inventions that he bought a rock drill and turned it into a machine-like robot. He called it *The Rock Drill* (1913).

☆ "VIRTUAL" ART

Some artists today use machines to create "virtual" art. This is made up of computer-generated forms and shapes called "fractals."

☆ PEOPLE OBJECTED TO THE CAMERA WHEN IT WAS INTRODUCED, BECAUSE THEY THOUGHT OF IT AS A MACHINE FOR MAKING ART.

☆ TATTOOS LAST FOR THE LIFETIME OF THE BODY THAT WEARS THEM. PATTERNS AND MOTIFS ARE PASSED DOWN FROM ONE GENERATION TO THE NEXT.

QUESTION 14

How is the human body used in art?

Body painting and tattooing are ancient forms of art. They are still popular today.

Connect! THE BODY HAS ALWAYS BEEN AN IMPORTANT SUBJECT FOR ARTISTS. SEE Q33.

☆ TATTOOS

Tattoos are made by pricking small holes in the skin with a sharp stick, bone or needle that has been coated in natural dyes. Shapes and symbols may have meanings or tell stories. Cave paintings made over 10,000 years ago show humans with tattoos. Around 2,400 years ago, nomads in China covered themselves with tattoos depicting wild animals, such as wolves, deer, large cats and even monsters.

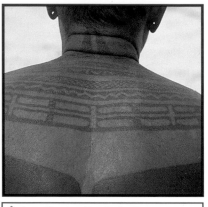
⬆ Some Maoris in New Zealand have covered themselves in elaborate tattoos.

☆ BODY PAINTING

All over the world, especially in African countries, painting the body with patterns and pictures has always been part of rituals and social festivals. Using make-up is also a kind of body painting.

☆ "HAPPENINGS"

When people use their bodies as part of a performance they may make works called "action art," "body art," or "happenings." **GILBERT** (born 1943) and **GEORGE** (born 1942) have worked together in London since 1968, making "actions"—that they call "sculptures"—and large "photo-pieces" as souvenirs of their performance art.

QUESTION 15

Is photography art?

Yes, when it is used not just to record the world, but also to show us new ways of looking at situations and scenes.

☆ PIONEERS

1839 DAGUERREOTYPE
THE FRENCH PAINTER **LOUIS JACQUES MANDÉ DAGUERRE** (1787-1851) FOUND A WAY OF FIXING REAL-LIFE IMAGES ONTO PAPER.

1839 PHOTOGRAPHIC NEGATIVE
THE ENGLISH ARCHAEOLOGIST AND TRANSLATOR **WILLIAM HENRY FOX TALBOT** (1800-77) HAD WORKED ON "DRAWING PAPER" SINCE 1833. SIX YEARS LATER, HE SHOWED HIS PHOTOGRAPHIC DRAWINGS TO THE WORLD.

QUESTION 16

What is collage?

Collages are made by selecting different materials and then arranging and fixing them to a backing.

In 1912, **PICASSO** attached a piece of cloth printed with imitation furniture canework to his work to indicate a chair. He wanted to introduce real elements into his work so that it did not become too abstract.

GEORGES BRAQUE (1882-1963) sometimes just used pasted-on pieces of paper to make "papiers collés."

Connect! HOW DID ONE ARTIST USE TORN PAPER IN A SPONTANEOUS WAY? SEE Q45.

QUESTION 17

Can art make people famous?

Yes!

Art may make the artist, the person who commissions the work (asks or pays for it to be made) or even the person portrayed in the work very famous.

ONE OF THE MOST FAMOUS PAINTINGS IN THE WORLD IS THE *MONA LISA*, WHICH WAS PAINTED BETWEEN 1503 AND 1506 BY THE ITALIAN ARTIST **LEONARDO DA VINCI** (1452-1519). IT SHOWS LISA DEL GIOCONDO. TODAY, THIS PAINTING HANGS IN THE LOUVRE MUSEUM IN PARIS. NEARLY 500 YEARS LATER THE PAINTER AND THE FACE IN THE PAINTING ARE STILL WELL-KNOWN. THE IMAGE HAS BEEN REPRODUCED AND USED ALL OVER THE WORLD.

Connect! SOME OF THE MOST FAMOUS ARTISTS HAVE DIED IN POVERTY. SEE Q47.

It's time to think about

making

art... why does it look like it does?

What is style?

Can you paint without a brush?

How do artists paint light?

If you want to find out the answers to all these
questions, just turn the page and move onto
PART TWO of your journey. - - - ✈

QUESTION

18 Why does art look like it does?

It depends on why the work is being made, who it is for, who will see it, and what materials are available. Let's look at some of the decisions that artists make when they work.

☆ SUBJECT | ☆ MEDIUM | ☆ COMPOSITION | ☆ COLOR | ☆ MOOD | ☆ MESSAGE

● WHAT IS MY SUBJECT OR THEME?
A PORTRAIT
A LANDSCAPE
AN OBJECT
AN EVENT
AN IMAGINATIVE
SUBJECT

● WHAT MEDIUM, OR MATERIALS, WILL I CHOOSE TO USE?
PAINT, CRAYON, COLLAGE, PHOTOGRAPHY, CONCRETE, WOOD

● HOW WILL I ARRANGE, OR COMPOSE, THE IMAGES AND FORMS?
● HOW BIG WILL IT BE?

● HOW CAN I USE COLOR TO GIVE MY WORK OF ART MOOD, MEANING AND SPIRIT?

● DOES THE WORK SHOW—OR EXPRESS—ANGER, SADNESS, PEACE OR HAPPINESS?

● WHAT AM I TRYING TO TELL PEOPLE ABOUT ME, THEM, THE WORLD, OR AN EVENT?

Prove It!

List the decisions you would make if you were going to represent your family. Think about your resources, such as space, materials, skills and time.

Connect! SOME ARTISTS USE UNUSUAL COLORS TO MAKE THE VIEWER REACT. SEE Q25.

QUESTION

19 What is style?

This is the way the art looks after the artist has finished making decisions.

STYLE IS LIKE A LANGUAGE MADE UP OF COLORS, SHAPES AND SYMBOLS. ARTISTS HAVE THEIR OWN UNIQUE STYLES.

STYLE IS INFLUENCED BY THE BELIEFS AND TRADITIONS OF THE SOCIETY IN WHICH THE ARTIST LIVES AND WORKS.

QUESTION

20 Who makes the rules?

Throughout history people have suggested that there are "right" ways of making art.

ARTISTS ARE INFLUENCED BY EACH OTHER, BY EVENTS HAPPENING IN THEIR WORLD, AND BY THEIR PATRONS. THE ITALIAN PAINTER **TITIAN** TRAINED WITH **GIOVANNI BELLINI** (1430–1516) AND WAS INSPIRED BY **GIORGIO BARBARELLI** (1478–1511).

☆ ACADEMIES

Academies were first set up in 16th-century Italy. This period is called The Renaissance, which means "rebirth" in French. It began in Italy in the 14th century and flourished in Europe from the early 15th century until the late 16th century. It centered around the style and subjects of the Greek and Roman classical world. Academies taught students ideas that suggested there was an ideal beauty and a correct way of making art.

Connect! SOME ARTISTS REJECTED THESE IDEAS IN THE 19TH CENTURY. SEE Q34.

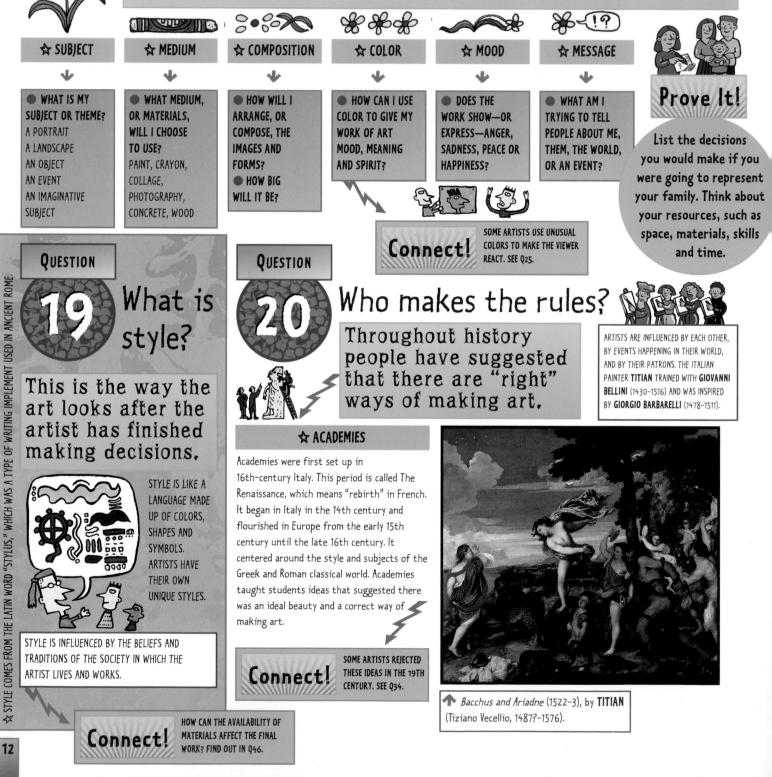

⬆ *Bacchus and Ariadne* (1522–3), by **TITIAN** (*Tiziano Vecellio, 1487?–1576*).

☆ STYLE COMES FROM THE LATIN WORD "STYLUS," WHICH WAS A TYPE OF WRITING IMPLEMENT USED IN ANCIENT ROME.

Connect! HOW CAN THE AVAILABILITY OF MATERIALS AFFECT THE FINAL WORK? FIND OUT IN Q46.

21 Why do we label styles of art?

Connect!
HOW DOES MONET USE COLOR TO SHOW LIGHT? FIND OUT IN Q26.

It makes it easier for us to look at art and learn from it.

Imagine if every piece of art ever made was scattered across a gigantic room. We'd never be able to see who made what, when and how. Artists themselves, and people who record changes in how art is made, such as historians and critics, often put art into different categories and then label them. This particularly happens in Western art.

Art movements may be named by critics (people who report on art events in newspapers and on the radio and television). Sometimes they have disliked a new style, only to find that their criticism has provided a name for the art group.

☆ SOME OF THE WORDS USED TO LABEL WESTERN ART

RENAISSANCE (14TH-16TH CENTURIES) INSPIRED BY CLASSICAL GREEK AND ROMAN ART, AND A WISH TO MAKE ART THAT LOOKED REAL.
KEY PLAYERS: LEONARDO DA VINCI, MICHELANGELO.

BAROQUE (17TH-18TH CENTURIES) INFLUENCED BY ROME AND NEW SCIENTIFIC DISCOVERIES.
KEY PLAYERS: PETER PAUL RUBENS, MICHELANGELO MERISI DA CARAVAGGIO, DIEGO RODRIGUEZ DE SILVA Y VELAZQUEZ.

ROMANTICISM (AROUND 1790-1830) INTERESTED IN AN IDEALIZED VIEW OF NATURE, THE PAST AND LEGENDARY HEROES.
KEY PLAYERS: JOHN CONSTABLE, JOSEPH MALLORD WILLIAM TURNER.

IMPRESSIONISM (LATE 19TH CENTURY) DEPICTED EVERYDAY SCENES AND TRIED TO CAPTURE THE CHANGING EFFECTS OF LIGHT.
KEY PLAYERS: CLAUDE MONET, PIERRE AUGUSTE RENOIR.

FUTURISM (1909-16) CAPTURED THE SPEED AND ENERGY OF THE MODERN WORLD, PARTICULARLY THE MACHINE AGE.
KEY PLAYERS: GINO SEVERINI, FILIPPO TOMMASO MARINETTI.

CUBISM (EARLY 20TH CENTURY) SHOWED DIFFERENT VIEWS OF AN OBJECT IN A SINGLE IMAGE BY BREAKING IT DOWN INTO GEOMETRIC SHAPES AND VIEWING IT FROM MORE THAN ONE ANGLE.
KEY PLAYERS: GEORGES BRAQUE, PABLO PICASSO.

SURREALISM (1920S AND 1930S) INSPIRED BY STRANGE AND EXTRAORDINARY THOUGHTS, DREAMS AND IMAGES, AND OFTEN MADE SPONTANEOUSLY.
KEY PLAYERS: SALVADOR DALI, MAX ERNST.

CONSTRUCTIVISM (FOUNDED IN 1915) SCULPTURES CREATED FROM MAN-MADE MATERIALS SUCH AS METAL AND PLASTIC.
KEY PLAYERS: NAUM GABO, VLADIMIR TATLIN.

EXPRESSIONISM (EARLY 20TH CENTURY) EXAGGERATED NATURAL APPEARANCES IN ORDER TO EXPRESS THE ARTIST'S EMOTIONS AND INNER VISION.
KEY PLAYERS: ERNST LUDWIG KIRCHNER, OSKAR KOKOSCHKA.

ABSTRACT EXPRESSIONISM (1940S) DEVELOPED IN NEW YORK, EMPHASIZING SPONTANEOUS PERSONAL EXPRESSION.
KEY PLAYERS: JACKSON POLLOCK, FRANZ KLINE.

POP ART (1960S) USED IMAGES OF THE MASS MEDIA, ADVERTISING AND POP CULTURE TO PRESENT EVERYDAY IMAGES AS ART.
KEY PLAYERS: ANDY WARHOL, ROY LICHTENSTEIN.

MINIMALISM (MID-1960S) EMPHASIS ON SIMPLICITY.
KEY PLAYERS: CARL ANDRE, FRANK STELLA.

☆ IMPRESSIONISM

Starting in 1863, the Salon des Refusés, Paris, showed the work of artists who had been rejected by the official salon. People found their rough painting techniques and haphazard colored patches alarming. In 1874, **CLAUDE MONET** exhibited a painting called *Impression, Sunrise*. The work was criticized for being "just an impression," but the artists adopted the word as a name for their group.

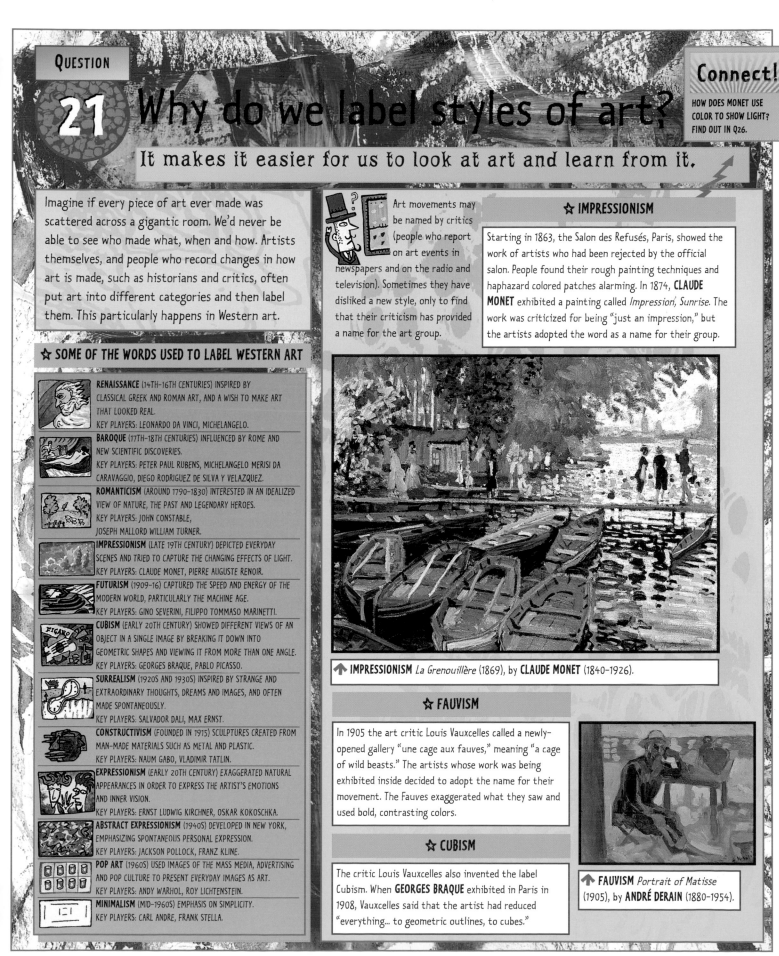

⬆ **IMPRESSIONISM** *La Grenouillère* (1869), by **CLAUDE MONET** (1840-1926).

☆ FAUVISM

In 1905 the art critic Louis Vauxcelles called a newly-opened gallery "une cage aux fauves," meaning "a cage of wild beasts." The artists whose work was being exhibited inside decided to adopt the name for their movement. The Fauves exaggerated what they saw and used bold, contrasting colors.

☆ CUBISM

The critic Louis Vauxcelles also invented the label Cubism. When **GEORGES BRAQUE** exhibited in Paris in 1908, Vauxcelles said that the artist had reduced "everything... to geometric outlines, to cubes."

⬆ **FAUVISM** *Portrait of Matisse* (1905), by **ANDRÉ DERAIN** (1880-1954).

☆ 20TH CENTURY ARTISTS HAVE BEEN OBSESSED BY PROGRESS AND INVENTION. ART THAT SEEMS MODERN AND NEW IS SOMETIMES CALLED **AVANT-GARDE**.

QUESTION

22 What is paint?

Paint is made from powdered colors, called pigments, or chemicals. It has been used for thousands of years by artists to make art.

Connect!

TURN TO Q31 TO SEE HOW SOME ARTISTS USE STONES AND ROCKS IN THEIR WORK.

☆ TYPES OF PAINT

● **OILS** Pigments are mixed with drying oils and thinned down with white spirit or turpentine.

● **WATER COLORS** Finely ground pigments are mixed with a gum. The paint is then sold in tubes or cakes.

● **GOUACHE** The pigment is made thicker by mixing it with white pigment or chalk.

● **ACRYLICS** Pigments are mixed with a binder based on an acrylic emulsion, and then sold in different forms, including tubes.

☆ MAKING PAINT FROM PIGMENTS

Pigments come from rocks, soil, plants, insects and shells. Some paints are made from chemicals.

1 THE PIGMENT IS GROUND DOWN UNTIL IT BECOMES A POWDER.

2 THE FINE POWDER IS MIXED, USING A PALETTE KNIFE OR MULLER, WITH A LIQUID (SUCH AS OIL, WATER, EGG OR GUM) TO BIND IT TOGETHER.

3 THE ARTIST MAY THEN MIX COLORS ON A THIN BOARD OR SLAB, CALLED A PALETTE, AND PAINT ONTO CARDBOARD, PAPER, WOOD OR A MATERIAL CALLED CANVAS.

Connect!

WHEN DID THE ACT OF PUTTING THE PAINT ONTO THE CANVAS BECOME MORE IMPORTANT THAN THE FINAL PAINTING? SEE Q24.

☆ PAINT IN TUBES

BY 1842, ARTISTS COULD BUY WATERCOLOR AND OIL PAINT IN TUBES, RATHER THAN HAVING TO MIX IT THEMSELVES. HOW DID THIS DEVELOPMENT CHANGE ART?

● **WHAT THEY PAINTED (THE SUBJECT) CHANGED.** IT WAS EASIER TO PAINT LANDSCAPES AND SCENES "EN PLEIN AIR"—OUTDOORS—BECAUSE PAINT IN TUBES STAYED MOIST AND WOULD LAST FOR DAYS. BEFORE THE INVENTION OF TUBES, COLORS WERE MIXED IN THE STUDIO AND CARRIED AROUND IN PIGS' BLADDERS.

● **HOW THEY PAINTED CHANGED.** IMPRESSIONIST ARTISTS MADE QUICK, VIVID PAINTINGS THAT LOOKED LIVELY BUT UNFINISHED. SOME ARTISTS USED PAINT STRAIGHT FROM THE TUBE, CREATING BOLD, BRIGHT PAINTINGS.

The strong brushwork and vivid colors of **VINCENT VAN GOGH**'s painting show the influences of Monet and the Impressionists.

☆ RECIPES FOR COLOR

ULTRAMARINE	USED TO BE MADE FROM LAPIS LAZULI, A SEMI-PRECIOUS STONE, BUT NOW MADE FROM CHEMICALS.
SCARLET	MADE FROM THE DRIED BLOOD OF THE MEXICAN COCHINEAL ANT.
INDIGO BLUE	MADE FROM TROPICAL PLANTS.
BURNT SIENNA	MADE FROM SOIL.
EMERALD GREEN	CONTAINS ARSENIC, A TYPE OF POISON.
TYRIAN PURPLE	MADE FROM CRUSHED SHELLFISH.

Danger!

SOME PAINT CAN KILL. THESE PAINTS CONTAIN POISONOUS SUBSTANCES.
● LEAD WHITE
● CHROME YELLOW
● CADMIUM RED
● VERMILION RED

Connect!

THE UNUSUAL PERSPECTIVE AND COMPOSITION SHOW THE ARTIST'S INTEREST IN JAPANESE ART. Q42 TELLS YOU MORE.

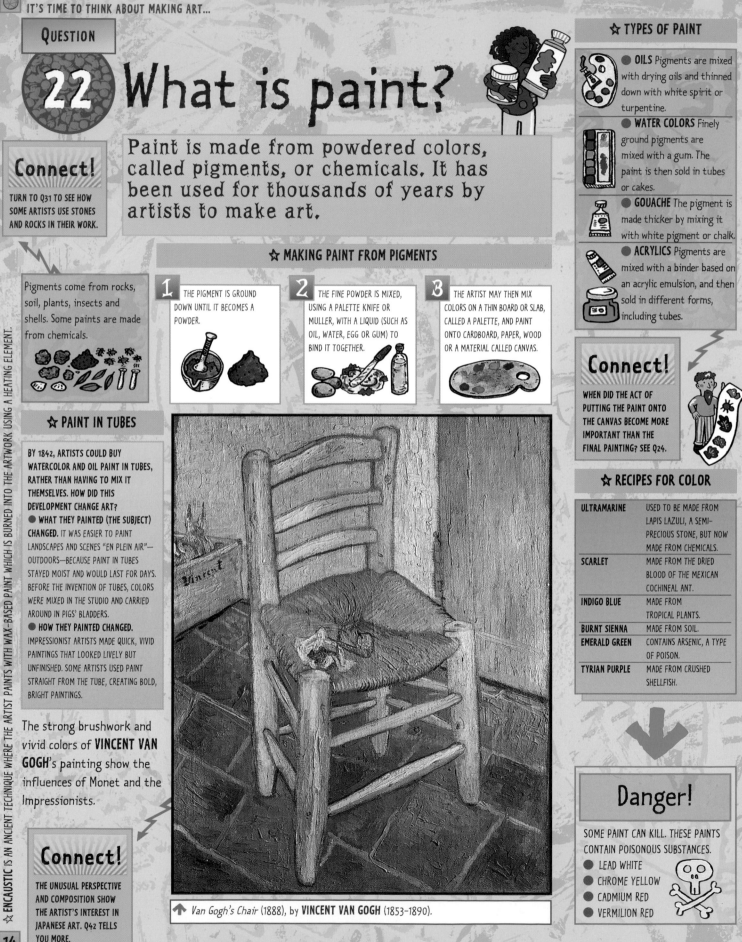

⬆ *Van Gogh's Chair* (1888), by **VINCENT VAN GOGH** (1853–1890).

☆ **ENCAUSTIC** IS AN ANCIENT TECHNIQUE WHERE THE ARTIST PAINTS WITH WAX-BASED PAINT WHICH IS BURNED INTO THE ARTWORK USING A HEATING ELEMENT.

QUESTION 23

Why was the invention of oil painting so important?

Oil paint changed the way artists could paint.

In Europe, from the 5th century until the 16th century, powdered paint was thickened with egg yolk and water. This process was called egg tempera. The paint dried very quickly. Early in the 1500s artists started to mix pigments with oil. This dried very slowly, allowing painters to keep working on the detail of the painting.

The Flemish painter **JAN VAN EYCK** was thought to have invented this new technique. Actually, oil paints had been used in the 8th century for painting onto stone and glass. But Van Eyck used oil paints in a completely new way that was to influence other artists for centuries.

EXAMINE THIS PAINTING
- VAN EYCK USED OIL PAINTS TO IMITATE THE SURFACE TEXTURES OF THE LITTLE DOG, THE BRASS OF THE CHANDELIER AND THE GLASS OF THE MIRROR.
- HE WORKED SLOWLY, SOMETIMES USING HIS FINGERTIPS. HIS FINGERPRINTS CAN BE DETECTED ON THE GREEN GOWN.
- HE PAINTED THE EFFECT OF LIGHT ENTERING THE ROOM THROUGH THE WINDOW AND FALLING ON OBJECTS.

⬆ *The Arnolfini Wedding* (1434), by **JAN VAN EYCK** (1390–1441).

Connect! WHO EXPERIMENTED WITH NEW WAYS OF PAINTING LIGHT? FIND OUT IN Q26.

QUESTION 24

Can you paint without a brush?

Yes, paint can be poured, dripped or splashed onto a canvas.

Prove It!

Make a work of art by dabbing paint onto paper with a sponge or vegetable. Try flicking it off a comb or painting with your thumbs.

☆ ACTION PAINTING

In New York in the 1940s and 1950s, artists such as **JACKSON POLLOCK** and **WILLEM DE KOONING** (born 1904) acted out how they felt as they made their work. The act of painting itself was the subject of the paintings. These artists were called Abstract Expressionists or "action painters." Pollock threw away his easel and palette, and tacked a canvas to the floor, or wall, onto which he dripped and splattered household paint from tins.

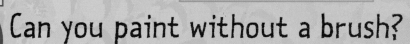

⬆ *Number 14* (1951), by **JACKSON POLLOCK** (1912–1956).

ARTISTS MAY FIND SOMETHING OTHER THAN A BRUSH TO PUT THE PAINT ONTO THE PAPER OR CANVAS.

☆ HUMAN BRUSHES

In the 1960s, the French painter **YVES KLEIN** (1928–62) made paintings by using human bodies as paintbrushes. Naked models were covered with paint, and their bodies then imprinted onto paper or canvas. This process was filmed.

Connect! CAN ART BE SHOCKING? CHECK OUT Q44.

15

QUESTION

25 How do artists use color?

Artists select combinations of colors to create special effects. How we see each color depends on the light that surrounds it and the colors next to it. When we look at a painting we are seeing all these colors together.

☆ THE COLOR WHEEL

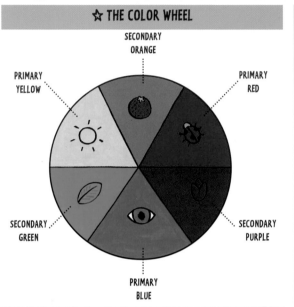

SECONDARY ORANGE

PRIMARY YELLOW

PRIMARY RED

SECONDARY GREEN

SECONDARY PURPLE

PRIMARY BLUE

PRIMARY COLORS = RED, YELLOW, AND BLUE. THESE COLORS CANNOT BE MADE BY MIXING ANY OTHER COLORS.

SECONDARY COLORS = ORANGE, GREEN, AND PURPLE. THESE COLORS ARE MADE BY MIXING TWO PRIMARY COLORS.

COMPLEMENTARY COLORS = EACH COLOR'S COMPLEMENTARY COLOR IS THE ONE OPPOSITE IT ON THE COLOR WHEEL: RED = GREEN; ORANGE = BLUE; YELLOW = PURPLE. WHEN PUT NEXT TO EACH OTHER THE COMPLEMENTARY COLORS SEEM TO JUMP OUT.

⬆ *Sunflowers* (1888), by **VINCENT VAN GOGH** (1853–1890).

Prove It!

Take an orange into strong sunlight and note its color. Now look at the orange under an electric light. The color of the fruit is changed by the light around it.

VINCENT VAN GOGH made four sunflower paintings between 1888 and 1889. He intended to display them around another painting of the wife of his friend. He felt that the yellow and orange tones of the flowers would make the green and red portrait look even more brilliant.

Prove It!

Colors can be linked to a feeling or a state of being—such as anger, sadness, happiness, or calmness. What do these colors suggest to you?

Connect!

THE BRIGHTNESS OF THESE COLORS SHOCKED PEOPLE AT THE TIME. TURN TO Q44 TO SEE HOW OTHER ARTISTS HAVE SHOCKED THE WORLD.

☆ COLOR AND MOOD

Artists use combinations of colors to show moods and feelings. In *Boating on the Seine*, **RENOIR** used bright colors straight from the tube and put complementary colors, such as orange and blue, next to each other. This makes the painting particularly vivid and the boat looks like it is moving on the shimmering water. Renoir also chose to use white and seven intensely colored paints—most of which had just been invented.

⬆ *Boating on the Seine* (1879–80), by **PIERRE AUGUSTE RENOIR** (1841–1919).

26 How do artists paint light?

Artists realized that to make objects look real they had to make them look solid. To do this, they studied the light as it hit the object—looking at the highlights (the brighter areas) and the shadows (the darker areas).

The Dutch artist **REMBRANDT VAN RIJN** (1606–1669) painted light and shadows by contrasting dark and bright areas. In *A Woman Bathing in a Stream* (1654), he created deep shadows by using pure black paint next to white and gray areas.

The French painter **CLAUDE MONET** wanted to show how light and atmosphere changed during the day. In *The Water-Lily Pond* (1899), he painted his oriental water garden in the sunlight of a summer's afternoon.

Connect!

MONET ADMIRED JAPANESE ART. HOW HAVE OTHER ARTISTS REACTED TO ART FROM DIFFERENT CULTURES? CHECK OUT Q42.

Connect!

HOW HAVE ARTISTS USED ELECTRIC LIGHT IN THEIR ART? SEE Q46.

27 How many ways are there to make a line?

Artists are limited only by their imagination, their materials and their time.

Prove It!

Make ten lines using objects and materials found in your home. Experiment with different colors, curves and thicknesses.

TWO-DIMENSIONAL LINE
USE A PENCIL, PEN, PASTEL, CRAYON OR BRUSH STROKE.

THREE-DIMENSIONAL LINE
MAKE A LINE OF STONES OR ANY OTHER SOLID OBJECT.

ELECTRONIC LINE
MAKE A LINE USING A COMPUTER.

TRY SOMETHING NEW
THE CHINESE LANDSCAPE PAINTERS OF THE 6TH CENTURY USED UNUSUAL TECHNIQUES, SUCH AS PAINTING WORKS OF ART WITH THEIR BARE FINGERS INSTEAD OF BRUSHES.

USE WHATEVER MATERIALS YOU HAVE
THE INUIT (OR ESKIMO) PEOPLE FROM THE NORTH-WEST COAST OF CANADA TRADITIONALLY MADE ART AND OBJECTS FROM WALRUS IVORY. THIS WAS ONCE ONE OF THE FEW MATERIALS AVAILABLE TO THEM.

Connect!

THE EXPLORERS WHO VISITED DISTANT LANDS FOUND EXTRAORDINARY ART. FIND OUT MORE IN Q41 AND Q42.

28 Is art all around us?

Yes. Some art is made to be seen and used every day. It may be beneath your feet, above your head or in your closet!

1 Art on walls...

Artists have decorated walls for thousands of years. A picture or design that adorns a wall is called a MURAL.

The ancient Egyptians made murals in tombs showing people, possessions and events that were important to the person buried there.

During the Roman Empire, between 27 BC and AD 476, many spectacular wall paintings were made, depicting temples, gardens, gods and heroes.

IN AD 79, VESUVIUS, AN ACTIVE VOLCANO NEAR NAPLES IN ITALY, ERUPTED. THE NEARBY CITIES OF POMPEII, STABIAE, AND HERCULANEUM WERE PRESERVED BY BEING BURIED IN LAYERS OF CINDERS, ASH AND STONE. THE ANCIENT ART AND ARCHITECTURE OF POMPEII WERE REDISCOVERED IN THE 1700S AFTER A PEASANT DIGGING IN A VINEYARD STRUCK A BURIED WALL.

☆ FRESCOES

A painting that is put onto the wet plaster of a wall is called a FRESCO (meaning "fresh" in Italian). As the plaster dries, the paint is fixed to the wall. Frescoes may feature columns, arches and windows, creating images which trick the eyes. This technique is called "trompe-l'oeil."

Connect!

Q40 REVEALS HOW AN ARTIST WORKING IN THE 13TH CENTURY USED FRESCOES TO TELL STORIES.

☆ WALL HANGINGS

The Bayeux Tapestry is a wall hanging that was made during the late 1000s. It is a 230 foot long strip of linen embroidered with colored wools. It tells the story, in pictures, of the Norman Conquest of England in 1066.

Connect!

WHAT EFFECT DID THE ART OF POMPEII HAVE ON ARTISTS WHEN IT WAS DISCOVERED? SEE Q41.

2 Art on floors...

Thousands of tiny pieces of colored stones may be embedded in floors to make patterns and pictures, which are called MOSAICS. Black and white mosaics were popular in the 1st century, especially in Rome. The invention of a waterproof cement into which the pieces could be fixed meant that many good examples have survived. Mosaics have also been made on walls and ceilings.

THE IMPRESSIONIST GEORGES SEURAT (1859–91) CREATED PAINTED MOSAICS. HIS TECHNIQUE WAS CALLED "POINTILLISM." IN HIS PAINTING CALLED A BATHING PLACE, ASNIÈRES (1884), TINY SPOTS OF COLOR ARE PAINTED ONTO A CANVAS. FROM A DISTANCE, THESE SEEM TO MERGE TOGETHER, APPEARING TO BE AREAS OF FLAT COLOR.

Many artists today create sculptures that they place directly on the floor, rather than on a base or pedestal. CARL ANDRE's 144 Magnesium Square (1969) is art that you can walk on.

3 Art on ceilings...

In 1473, Pope Sixtus IV started to build the Sistine Chapel in the Vatican, Rome. In 1508, his nephew Pope Julius II asked **MICHELANGELO BUONARROTI** (1475-1564) to create a painting for the ceiling of the Sistine Chapel. It took him four years to complete.

Connect! ART TELLING RELIGIOUS STORIES HAS BEEN MADE BY MANY CULTURES AND IN MANY WAYS. CHECK OUT Q40.

4 Art in windows...

The Middle Ages in Europe was the time from the 5th century to the 16th century. Christianity was the foremost religion and many impressive churches were built, with elaborate stained glass windows telling religious stories. In AD 330, the Roman Emperor Constantine declared Byzantium—Istanbul in Turkey today—the capital of his empire, so art made in this time is often called **BYZANTINE** art.

STAINED GLASS IS COLORED BY ADDING DIFFERENT OXIDES DURING THE GLASS-MAKING PROCESS:
COBALT OXIDE = BLUE
COPPER OXIDE = RED
NICKEL OXIDE = PURPLE

⬆ This stained glass window in Chartres Cathedral, France, was made around 1210.

5 Art we wear...

The choice of color, design and materials may be significant if the item is to be worn on ceremonial occasions or in battle. This Hawaiian cloak, worn by chiefs, was made in the 18th century from red and yellow feathers.

6 Art we read...

Artists have created elaborate books and documents, that tell us about the customs, beliefs and life of the time. **MANUSCRIPTS** were produced on parchment or vellum, that is made from the skins of sheep, goats or calves. The tradition of making decorative and beautiful art books continues today.

Papyrus—made from the stem of the tall reeds that grew in the swamps of the Nile River—was used to create manuscripts as long ago as 2700 BC in ancient Egypt and Greece.

In Europe in the Middle Ages, especially in the late 700s and 800s, monks assisted by scribes produced **ILLUMINATED MANUSCRIPTS**. Initial letters and borders were decorated with gold and silver leaf.

⬆ The Book of Kells was made in Ireland between the mid-700s and early 800s. This illuminated manuscript tells the stories of the Christian Bible.

☆ ART & LANGUAGE

IN THE 1960S, A GROUP OF ARTISTS CALLED **ART & LANGUAGE**, LED BY TERRY ATKINSON, USED PRINTED MATERIAL, BOOKS AND WORDS TO PRESENT THEIR IDEA: THAT A WORK OF ART COULD BE A WRITTEN DISCUSSION ABOUT ART ITSELF. TODAY ARTISTS USE LETTERING, WORDS AND DESIGN TO SEND MESSAGES TO THE VIEWER.

⬆ Nigredo (1994), by **RICHARD MAKIN**, who is a writer and visual artist.

Connect! THE INVENTION OF PRINTING CHANGED ART. FIND OUT HOW IN Q41.

29 Some things have been the subject of art for centuries—what are they?

Animals, nature and the landscape...

THE FIRST PAINTINGS MADE BY PREHISTORIC PEOPLE WERE OF ANIMALS, AND ARTISTS HAVE FEATURED ANIMALS IN THEIR WORK EVER SINCE.

ARTISTS HAVE BEEN FASCINATED BY NATURE AND THE PLANET FOR THOUSANDS OF YEARS. THEY STUDY IT, DEPICT IT AND USE ITS RESOURCES.

EXAMINING ART SHOWS US WHAT PEOPLE FROM THE PAST AND FROM OTHER CULTURES LOOKED LIKE, WHAT THEY BELIEVED IN AND HOW THEY LIVED.

30 Why make art about animals?

Animals have always been important to humans as food, as pets, as status symbols and as symbols of their gods.

Prove It!

Make a work of art that shows how you feel about either a pet or a wild animal. What does it look like? Is it dangerous? What does it eat? Do you like it?

☆ ANIMALS AND SURVIVAL

Like artists today, early artists depicted what was important to them – animals. After the Pleistocene Ice Age (between 2 million and 10,000 years ago) our ancestors survived by hunting large herds of animals. These had been driven south by the cold into the areas that are known today as Spain and France.

☆ ANIMALS AND ANATOMY

The artist **GEORGE STUBBS** was fascinated by the world of horse racing and hunting. He was so determined to paint animals faithfully that he dissected them to study how their bodies were put together. He taught himself engraving so that he could publish *The Anatomy of the Horse*.

☆ ANIMALS AND MESSAGES

DAMIEN HIRST is a British artist who shocked the world by presenting sculptures that use real animals. The dead creatures are suspended in glass cubes containing a chemical called formaldehyde, that preserves the flesh. He aims to encourage people to think about life and death.

☆ ANIMALS AND BELIEF

Egyptian gods were often represented by animals, or part-animal and part-human creatures. In the 7th century sacred animal sculptures were cast in bronze. *The Gayer-Anderson Cat*, that represents the goddess Bastet, is hollow and has gold earrings. Today, some cultures still believe that species from the natural world have spirits.

↑ *The Milbanke and Melbourne Families* (1769), by **GEORGE STUBBS** (1724–1806).

↑ *Mother and Child Divided* (1993), by **DAMIEN HIRST** (born in 1965).

BRITISH ARTIST **MARK WALLINGER** (BORN IN 1959) HAS CREATED AN ART PROJECT CALLED *A REAL WORK OF ART*. IN THIS HE USES A REAL HORSE TO TELL PEOPLE HOW HE FEELS ABOUT THE WAY WE LIVE AND HOW WE BEHAVE TOWARDS EACH OTHER. HE ACTUALLY BOUGHT, TRAINED AND RODE A RACEHORSE THAT HE NAMED "A REAL WORK OF ART."

Connect!

SOME ARTISTS BECOME CELEBRITIES. FIND OUT MORE IN Q36.

31 How have artists shown what they feel about nature?

Connect!

HOW HAS OUR EXPLORATION OF THE PLANET INFLUENCED SOME ARTISTS? SEE Q41 AND Q42.

Earth has existed for at least 4 ½ billion years. *Homo sapiens sapiens* arrived around 40,000 years ago. Since then we have used nature as a subject, a place to put art and as a source for materials.

☆ **STONEHENGE**

BETWEEN 2800 BC AND 1500 BC, 19 PIECES OF SANDSTONE WERE HAULED OVER 186 MI TO THE SALISBURY PLAIN IN ENGLAND, TO MAKE STONEHENGE. THE POSITION OF THE STONES MAY RELATE TO THE MOVEMENTS OF THE SUN AND MOON.

☆ ANDY GOLDSWORTHY LET A SNOWBALL MELT ONTO PAPER. THE MARK IT MADE AND THE MELTING EVENT ITSELF BECAME A PIECE OF ART CALLED *SOURCE OF SCAUR*.

☆ THE SEA

Around 1700 BC, Greek palaces were made with frescoes showing marine and plant life. Pottery decorated with sea creatures has also been found.

JOSEPH MALLORD WILLIAM TURNER (1775–1851) was famous for creating dramatic, almost abstract, landscapes and sea paintings, such as *The Fighting Téméraire* (1838).

☆ THE LAND

JOHN CONSTABLE loved the English landscape. He painted it and wrote about it with passion.

⬆ *The Hay Wain* (1821), by **JOHN CONSTABLE** (1776–1837).

THE FRENCH PAINTER **JEAN-BAPTISTE CAMILLE COROT** (1796–1875) PAINTED OUTDOORS AND REVOLUTIONIZED THE WAY ARTISTS SAW NATURE. HIS LANDSCAPES WERE PEACEFUL AND OFTEN SHOWED PEASANTS AND WORKERS ENJOYING THE LAND.

☆ THE MATERIALS

Since the 1960s, **RICHARD LONG** (born in 1945) has gone on solitary walks all over the world. His art is the experience of the walk and he explains the events using maps, words and photographs. In the 1970s he made sculptures, such as *Slate Circle*, using stones and materials collected on his walks.

Connect!

GO TO Q35 TO SEE THE WAYS IN WHICH ART SHOWS US HOW THE WORLD HAS CHANGED.

QUESTION

32 Can nature and the climate destroy art?

Yes...

SCULPTURES AND MONUMENTS MAY BE WORN AWAY BY:

● **WEATHERING** Carbon dioxide in raindrops may attack and dissolve the surface of stone sculptures. Mosses and lichens can produce acids that eat into stone surfaces.

● **ACID RAIN** Burning coal and oil releases gases such as sulfur and nitrogen, which combine with the raindrops and make them acidic. Acid rain can destroy sculptures.

HARSH SUNLIGHT MAY MAKE THE COLORS IN PAINTINGS AND DRAWINGS FADE. ART GALLERIES USUALLY HAVE SUBDUED LIGHTING TO PROTECT PRECIOUS WORKS OF ART.

⬆ The surface of this sculpture has been attacked by acid rain.

33 How is art used to record the human body?

Hand prints dating back to 18,000 BC have been found in caves. Red, yellow and black paint was blown over outstretched hands to make the images. Artists have used the human body as a subject for thousands of years.

A 4.5-inch-high model of a woman was found in Austria. It is around 30,000 years old, and is made from limestone. This is one of the earliest examples of artists making models of the body.

☆ MAKING ART "FROM LIFE"

In ancient Greece, Rome and Egypt, portraits were made "from life"—real people were used as models. "Likenesses" were made so that people would be remembered after they had died. From around 1500, artists became more interested in the human body as subject matter. **MICHELANGELO** and **LEONARDO DA VINCI** were dissecting corpses to find out more about the way bodies worked. By the late 19th century, artists were depicting scenes from everyday life and many images were made by posing models in the studio.

ANTONY GORMLEY uses lead to make molds of his own body. He then creates sculptures. The artist is trying to tell people how he feels about being human.

⬆ *Untitled (for Francis)* (1985), by **ANTONY GORMLEY** (born in 1950).

⬆ *After the Bath, Woman Drying Herself* (1880s), by **HILAIRE GERMAIN EDGAR DEGAS** (1834-1917).

Connect! TURN TO Q37 TO SEE HOW WOMEN HAVE BEEN PORTRAYED IN ART.

34 Where else have artists looked for inspiration?

Artists are often influenced by studying the way people with different experiences make art.

☆ LOOKING TO THE PAST

The Pre-Raphaelite Brotherhood (PRB) was a secret society formed in 1848 by a number of artists who wanted to look to the past, study nature, and throw away the ideas and rules of the present art styles. **SIR JOHN EVERETT MILLAIS** (1829-96) spent nearly four months out of doors painting the nature scenes in *Ophelia* (1852). He wanted to be "true to nature." He added the figure to the background in the studio.

☆ CHILDREN'S ART

Artists have tried to capture in their work the freshness and liveliness that they see in children's art. The Swiss painter **PAUL KLEE** (1879-1940) was interested in dreams, fairytales and children's art. His work appears quite magical.

☆ ART FROM DIFFERENT CULTURES

At the beginning of the 20th century, museums expanded their displays of art from other cultures. Many artists were influenced by what they saw. **WASSILY KANDINSKY** (1866-1944) was a Russian artist who painted one of the first abstract paintings around 1913. It was called *Improvisations*. He was influenced by the simple boldness of what was called "primitive" art.

Connect! TURN TO Q43 TO SEE THE IMPACT THAT SO-CALLED "PRIMITIVE ART" HAD ON WESTERN ARTISTS.

Art makes an

impact!

Can art be shocking?

How does art make money? (AND WHO FOR?)

How does art bring people together?

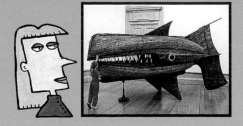

To find out how artists and their work
affect and reflect the world, turn the page to
PART THREE. --->

QUESTION

35 When we look at art, how can we see how the world has changed?

We can look at what art was made when, where and how.

Ask yourself...

1 WHY WAS THE ART MADE? →

3 DID SOMEONE PAY FOR IT TO BE MADE? →

2 WHAT IS THE SUBJECT? →

4 WHAT DOES IT LOOK LIKE? →

● Up until the 16th century, most Western art was made to decorate churches or royal courts. Artists told religious or historical stories in huge frescoes and altarpieces.

● Today, anyone with an idea, some skill and imagination may choose to be an artist. They make art any time and anywhere, and their works of art take on all kinds of shapes, sizes and forms.

☆ PATRONS

Western artists may have had patrons who paid them to carry out specific work. Pope Julius II was a patron to **RAPHAEL** (Raffaello Sanzio, 1483–1520). He asked him to paint frescoes in his private quarters in the Vatican.

⬆ One of **RAPHAEL**'s Vatican wall paintings (1510–11).

IN THE 16TH CENTURY, MICHELANGELO AND RAPHAEL WERE GREAT RIVALS AND VERY COMPETITIVE. MICHELANGELO THOUGHT RAPHAEL GOT ALL HIS IDEAS FROM LOOKING AT MICHELANGELO'S WORK IN THE SISTINE CHAPEL!

QUESTION

36 Do all artists show their true feelings in their work?

Artists used to be anonymous—they were not employed to express their own feelings. Now, some do present their opinions in their work.

DOCUMENTS SHOW THAT SCULPTORS WORKING FOR THE KING OF BABYLON IN 1275-1250 BC WERE TREATED AS ROYAL SERVANTS.

Connect!

SOME ARTISTS HAVE USED THEIR ART TO COMMENT ON THE WORLD. SEE Q38.

☆ ARTISTS AND FANTASY

HIERONYMUS BOSCH, a painter from the Netherlands, painted horrific fantasy paintings that shocked people at the time. He used his art to say that the human soul was in a sorry state.

⬆ *The Garden of Earthly Delights* (1500), by **HIERONYMUS BOSCH** (1450?–1516).

☆ WE CAN SEE ARTISTS BECOMING MORE AWARE OF THEIR POSITION WHEN THEY STARTED TO MAKE SELF-PORTRAITS AND INCLUDED THEMSELVES IN THEIR PAINTINGS.

37 What does art teach us about women?

Art reflects the changes in the way people look, as well as their position in society.

☆ HOW HAVE WOMEN BEEN PORTRAYED IN ART?

Around 30,000 years ago, tiny figures of women were carved out of stone. They were probably a kind of magic charm.

Chinese scrolls show court ladies getting advice on how to behave (AD 232-309).

Servant girls are seen waiting on the Indian god Krishna in *Krishna and the Maidens* (1710).

⬆ *Woman in a Multicolored Hat* (1939), by **PABLO PICASSO** (1881-1973).
Picasso distorted the features of the face of Dora Maar. This image is not about reflecting the model's beauty. The artist used her face to explore his own feelings, and different styles and techniques.

☆ HAVE WOMEN MADE ART?

Yes. But although there have been women artists, much of their work was not recorded by art historians. Women have also made art that was not hung in museums and galleries, such as embroidery and patchwork quilts. Today, some artists use traditional methods to deliver messages through their art.

⬆ *Spanking New Brunette*, detail (1993), by **SARAH FORRESTER** (born in 1965).

⬆ *Construccion*, by **FRIDA KAHLO** (1907-1954). Frida Kahlo was a famous Mexican artist who recorded her own experiences and feelings in her art. She often made self-portraits, and used symbols and the words of popular songs. She endured many operations after a serious accident, and much of her work is about anger and courage.

Connect! PEOPLE COME TOGETHER TO SEE ART. SEE Q49.

☆ ARTISTS ALIENATED FROM SOCIETY

The Norwegian painter **EDVARD MUNCH** left Norway in 1889 and traveled to Paris. He was a pessimistic and sometimes depressed man. His painting called *The Scream* shows his despair. He wrote of it: "I stood there trembling with fear and I felt a loud, unending scream piercing nature."

⬆ *The Scream* (1893), by **EDVARD MUNCH** (1863-1944).

☆ ART AS A 'CALLING' OR WAY OF LIFE

The French artist **PAUL GAUGUIN** was willing to leave his wife and children to travel to Tahiti, an island in the South Pacific, in 1891 to make art that he felt was unspoilt by "modern life."

⬆ *Faa Iheihe*, detail (1898), by **PAUL GAUGUIN** (1848-1903).

☆ ARTISTS AS CELEBRITIES

Some artists have become as famous as their work. **ANDY WARHOL** was an American pop artist who was always surrounded by artists and writers in his studio. Many of Warhol's most famous works consist of repeated images of movie stars such as Marilyn Monroe.

⬆ *Marilyn* (1967), by **ANDY WARHOL** (1930?-87).

Connect! SOME ARTISTS DIE VERY POOR WHILE OTHERS MAKE LOADS OF MONEY. FIND OUT MORE IN Q47.

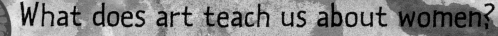
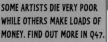

QUESTION

38 What does art tell us about history?

Artists record events, retell stories and often make powerful art to reflect their feelings and opinions.

War

Guernica, a town in northern Spain, was bombed in 1937 by German planes during the Spanish Civil War. Many innocent people were killed. One of the most famous and dramatic images of war is **PABLO PICASSO**'s 1937 painting *Guernica*, which shows the horror the artist felt at the bombing.

⬆ *Guernica* (1937), by **PABLO PICASSO** (1881–1973).

OFFICIAL WAR ARTISTS ARE OFTEN EMPLOYED TO RECORD EVENTS. **JOHN KEANE** WAS SENT TO THE GULF WAR IN 1990. **W. EUGENE SMITH** AND **DON McCULLIN** ARE TWO PHOTOGRAPHERS WHO SHOOK THE WORLD WITH THEIR IMAGES OF WAR.

Revolution

The French painter, **EUGÈNE DELACROIX** realized how important the French Revolution in 1789 was. Most of the royal family lost their heads at the guillotine and, with the monarchy disposed of, the French people were able to govern themselves. To show his excitement at this new-found freedom, Delacroix painted *Liberty Leading the People*.

⬆ *Liberty Leading the People* (1830), by **EUGÈNE DELACROIX** (1798–1863).

Connect! HOW DOES ART SHOW US WHAT PEOPLE BELIEVE IN? SEE Q40.

QUESTION

39 Does art borrow from everyday life?

Art may borrow ideas and images from print advertising, television and other aspects of our daily lives.

☆ POP ART

Pop art, a style that was popular in the 1960s, took images from comic books, advertising and packaging and manipulated them, turning them into art. Pop artists, such as **RICHARD HAMILTON** (born in 1922), wanted to make art "young, witty and gimmicky." The American pop artist **ROY LICHTENSTEIN** was interested in the way comics often took emotional subjects and presented them in a remote and deadpan way.

I PRESSED THE FIRE CONTROL... AND AHEAD OF ME ROCKETS BLAZED THROUGH THE SKY...

WHAAM!

⬆ *Whaam!* (1963), by **ROY LICHTENSTEIN** (born 1923).

☆ RECYCLING

SOME ARTISTS IN MEXICO USE TIN CANS AND OTHER MASS-PRODUCED ITEMS TO MAKE SCULPTURES AND MASKS. THESE BECOME A PART OF THEIR "DAY OF THE DEAD" FESTIVAL.

Connect! WHICH ARTIST IS FAMOUS FOR EXHIBITING "FOUND OBJECTS"? FIND OUT IN Q44.

☆ AMERICAN POP ARTIST **CLAES OLDENBURG** (BORN IN 1929) MADE GIGANTIC SOFT SCULPTURES OF EVERYDAY THINGS, INCLUDING HAMBURGERS AND LIPSTICK TUBES. THIS BROUGHT NEW MEANING TO OBJECTS WE NORMALLY TAKE FOR GRANTED.

40 What does art tell us about religion and beliefs?

We must look at the way artists have represented their gods and the religious stories that they tell in their art.

☆ CHRISTIANITY

1 From AD 64 to AD 313, it was illegal to be a Christian in the Roman Empire. Artists painted scenes in the Roman style but included symbols that were recognized by other believers. Christ was represented by a shepherd, a lamb or a cross.

2 In the AD 500s, the icon (a recognizable portrait of the Christian god) developed as a special kind of religious image in Byzantine art.

3 In AD 726, Emperor Leo III ordered all the icons to be destroyed because it was thought wrong to worship a likeness – especially if you believed that god actually lived in the painting. This belief lasted for 117 years.

↑ *The Pentecost* (about 1306-12), by **GIOTTO DI BONDONE** (1267?-1337). The Italian painter **GIOTTO DI BONDONE** was famous for making his paintings look realistic and three-dimensional. His frescoes in churches in Florence and Padua told elaborate stories and influenced many artists, including Michelangelo.

↑ *Christ before the High Priest* (about 1617), by **GERRIT VAN HONTHORST** (1590-1656). The artist used candlelight and darkness to make the work dramatic. The lighting emphasized the poses and expressions.

4 By the 16th century artists were using new techniques such as chiaroscuro—emphasizing light and shade—to make objects look three-dimensional.

5 Today, people can buy pictures of the Christian god in churches and shops all over the world.

☆ ISLAM AND JUDAISM

These religions forbid their followers to create images of living things. Muslim religious art mainly features geometric patterns.

Connect! CAN ART CHANGE WHAT PEOPLE BELIEVE? SEE Q42.

☆ BUDDHISM

Early Buddhist artists showed their leader and teacher, Siddhartha Gautama (563?-483? BC), as an abstract symbol. He was often depicted as a wheel, or a symbol of birth, growing older and dying. In the 3rd century AD, images of Buddha started to take on a human form. He was usually seen sitting cross-legged. Today, there are Buddhists all over the world, with large numbers in China, India and south-east Asia.

↑ A statue of a Buddha from Tibet, made in the 18th century.

☆ HINDUISM

The Hindu religion uses art to show its many gods, including Ganesh, the elephant-headed god, and Shiva, the four-armed god of life and death.

☆ SPIRITS

For thousands of years people have made images that represent the different spirits, gods and goddesses that they believe in. This pot was made in Mexico, about 700 years ago. The woman represents a god of life and the land.

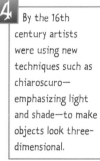

How do ideas spread across the world?

Explorers, traders, traveling craftsmen and artists have introduced people to the ideas of other cultures. Advances in technology have also spread techniques and theories.

☆ EXPLORERS

1492 CHRISTOPHER COLUMBUS (1451-1506), AN ITALIAN EXPLORER, TRIED TO SAIL TO ASIA BY SAILING WESTWARDS. INSTEAD HE DISCOVERED THE "NEW WORLD" OF AMERICA.

1497-9 THE PORTUGUESE NAVIGATOR VASCO DA GAMA (1469?-1524) TRAVELED BY SEA FROM AFRICA TO INDIA.

1520 MEXICO WAS CONQUERED BY THE SPANISH, AND GOLD, SILVER AND ART MADE FROM FEATHERS WAS SENT BY HERNANDO CORTÉS (1485-1547) FROM MEXICO TO KING CHARLES I.

☆ ARCHAEOLOGY

Pompeii, buried when Vesuvius erupted in AD 79, was rediscovered in 1748. Wall-paintings, mosaics and personal possessions gave artists an insight into Roman art and led to the development of a Classical art style in Europe in the 18th century.

☆ PRINTING

The type mold was invented by **JOHANNES GUTENBERG** (1395?-1468?) in the 1400s. This meant that books and art prints could be distributed in large quantities. The German artist **ALBRECHT DURER** became famous for his prints.

☆ PHOTOGRAPHY

When photography was invented in 1826, artists could experiment with color, light and abstract forms, presenting new ways to look at old subjects. Art could now be reproduced and in the 1890s many international art magazines were set up.

☆ RADIO AND TELEVISION

Radio, invented in 1895, and television, invented in 1926, allow ideas to travel across the world very quickly. Art styles can be observed, theories debated and techniques shared. Some artists become very famous.

↑ *The Last Supper* (1527), by **ALBRECHT DURER** (1471-1528).

Connect!

HOW IS TELEVISION USED IN ART TODAY? TURN TO Q46.

How were Western artists influenced by art from other cultures?

Europeans believed that their rules about style and subject matter were the best ones. Art from China and Japan revolutionized these ideas.

☆ AZTEC AND INCA

The Aztec founded Tenochtitlan (on the site of present-day Mexico City) in about 1325. They built palaces and pyramids and made impressive stone carvings and sculptures. The Inca expanded their rule in Peru in about 1200 and made textiles and pottery.

When small armies of Spaniards conquered these cultures in the 16th century, the idea that Europe was "born to rule" spread, strengthening the belief that European ideas in art were the best ones.

☆ CHINA

Genghis Khan and the Mongols conquered China in the early 1200s. His grandson, Kublai, made himself emperor of the Yuan dynasty in 1279. Marco Polo, travelling around Asia between 1271 and 1295, shipped silks and artifacts to Europe, where styles were imitated by artists and craftsmen. Heavy taxes, starvation and rebellion forced the Mongols to leave China in 1368.

☆ IN 1911-1914 A GROUP CALLED **DER BLAUE REITER** EXPLORED ABORIGINAL ART, ART FROM EASTER ISLAND, BRAZIL AND MEXICO, RUSSIAN FOLK ART AND CHILDREN'S PAINTINGS AND DRAWINGS.

43

Was African art particularly influential?

Yes. In the early 20th century the look and style of African masks and sculptures inspired Picasso and many others.

PABLO PICASSO collected African masks and sculptures. He felt they showed him that he did not have to paint what he saw, but what he felt and knew of the subject. The German artist **EMIL NOLDE** was fascinated by the strength and simplicity of African art.

⬆ *Les Demoiselles d'Avignon* (1907), by **PABLO PICASSO**.

⬆ *Masks* (1911), by **EMIL NOLDE** (1867–1956).

⬆ An African ceremonial mask from the Congo, made by the Zombo tribe.

☆ JAPAN

From the mid-1600s to the mid-1800s, prints called ukiyo-e flourished in Japan. They showed everyday scenes, including bathhouses and fashionable women. This art explored a new way of seeing the world and European artists were impressed. **DEGAS** hung examples above his bed. **MONET** admired the freshness and brightness of color, the strange compositions and scenes of everyday life. **VAN GOGH** and **GAUGUIN** were inspired by the bold shapes, strong line and lack of shadows and perspective. The French artist **TOULOUSE-LAUTREC** copied the flatness and boldness of line and color in his posters.

⬆ A Japanese ukiyo-e print by **BUNCHO** (1725–94).

⬆ *At the Moulin Rouge*, detail (1892), by **HENRI DE TOULOUSE-LAUTREC** (1864–1901).

44

Can art shock?

Yes.

THE ARMORY SHOW, held in New York in 1913, displayed work by **VAN GOGH**, **GAUGUIN** and **PICASSO**. The revolutionary style of this work changed art in America forever.

DADAISM was an art movement founded in Switzerland in 1916, which aggressively mocked traditions and so-called "good taste." The artists wrote manifestos and staged events that alarmed many people. The French artist **MARCEL DUCHAMP** produced "ready-mades"—art made out of everyday objects. *Fountain* was shocking because it was made out of a public urinal. Duchamp was trying to say that art was not what you saw, but what you thought when you looked at it.

⬆ *Fountain* (1917), by **MARCEL DUCHAMP** (1887–1968).

Connect!

SEE HOW SOME UNUSUAL ART FORMS HAVE BROUGHT PEOPLE TOGETHER IN Q49.

45 Can art be spontaneous?

Yes. Some artists may be more inspired by chance events and dreams than rules and traditions.

☆ SURREALISM

The Surrealists made art inspired by their dreams, imagination and memories. They discussed ideas in manifestos and in 1925 held their first exhibition in Paris.

⬆ *The Disintegration of the Persistence of Memory* (1952–4), by **SALVADOR DALI** (1904–89).

☆ AUTOMATISM

This style of art encouraged the artist to act subconsciously, or without thinking. The French artist **JEAN (HANS) ARP** (1887–1966) threw torn-up pieces of paper on the floor. The random patterns the paper made became his collage.

Prove It!

Tear sheets of colored paper into small pieces. Throw them onto a sheet of paper covered with glue. Whatever sticks to your glued paper forms your collage.

---

46 What is the link between art and science?

The ways in which we make art and see the world have been influenced by inventions and scientific discoveries.

☆ CONSERVATION

TRAINED SCIENTISTS WORK TO CONSERVE ART SO THAT IT DOES NOT DISINTEGRATE WITH AGE.

⬆ Conserving an Egyptian wall painting.

1 THE WORK IS CLEANED AND STABILIZED IN ORDER TO STOP ANY FURTHER DECAY. CHEMICALS FROM THE ATMOSPHERE ATTACK PAPER AND STONE.

2 THE WORK MIGHT BE FRAGILE AND CLEANING IT MUST NOT REMOVE EVIDENCE OF THE USE OF THE OBJECT – FOR EXAMPLE, FOOD REMAINS OR TRACES OF SMOKE ARE LEFT IN PLACE.

3 THE WORK IS RESTORED. BLEMISHES ARE CAMOUFLAGED AND FRESH PAINT ADDED WHERE NECESSARY.

☆ NEW COLORS

In the 15th century Italian craftsmen kept their paint-making formulas secret. In the 19th century, machines were invented that allowed paint to be made in large quantities. In the last hundred years new synthetic and artificial pigments have been developed to meet the demands of industry and artists.

THE BRIGHT YELLOW PAINT THAT **TURNER** USED IN HIS PAINTING *THE FIGHTING TÉMÉRAIRE* (1838) HAD ONLY JUST BECOME AVAILABLE.

☆ NEW MATERIALS

The Constructivists working in Russia around 1915 were inspired by machine-made materials. **VLADIMIR TATLIN** (1885–1953) made sculptures from glass, tin and plaster. Some artists in the 1960s used new inventions in their art, such as fluorescent light bulbs.

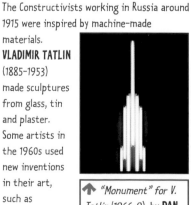

⬆ *"Monument" for V. Tatlin* (1966–9), by **DAN FLAVIN** (born in 1933).

☆ NEW METHODS

Photography, television and video have helped artists communicate difficult and complicated ideas to an audience by using a medium that people recognize.

⬆ **NAM JUNE PAIK** (born in 1932) uses 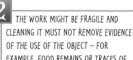 television sets in his sculptures.

47 How does art make money?

(AND WHO FOR?)

Art makes money when it is bought and sold.

When art started to be exhibited, people wanted to buy it. So art was given a value. Today, dealers and gallery owners often decide how much art is worth. They keep some of the sale price and the artist usually receives the rest. The more famous the artist, the higher the value of his or her work.

☆ THE RICH

PABLO PICASSO made around 13,500 paintings and designs, 100,000 prints and engravings, 34,000 book illustrations and 300 sculptures. His complete work is estimated to be worth more than $765 million.

☆ THE POOR

VINCENT VAN GOGH became an artist in 1881. He felt it was his "calling." He was very depressed and spent time in an asylum. The artist killed himself in 1890, but in the last 70 days of his life he painted 70 canvasses. Van Gogh sold only one painting during his lifetime and died poor and unknown. Now his paintings sell for up to $75 million.

☆ ONE OF THE MOST VALUABLE PAINTINGS IS THE *MONA LISA* (1503–6) BY **LEONARDO DA VINCI** (1452–1519). IT IS INSURED FOR $107 MILLION.

48 What is a forgery?

A forgery is a copy of the style of a specific artist, usually using the same materials and techniques.

IS THIS WRONG? →

● **YES** if the work of art gives a false impression about who has made it.
● **YES** if it has been bought because of its value, so that it can be resold as the work of a known artist.
● **NO** if the work is bought by someone who appreciates it and knows that it has not been made by a famous artist.

49 How does art bring people together?

Art can be a public event. It may also intrigue or outrage society.

☆ PEOPLE ARE UNITED

In 1958, the Bulgarian artist **CHRISTO** (Christo Jaracheff, born in 1935) began wrapping up objects and calling them sculptures. In 1995, Christo and his wife Marie-Claude wrapped the Reichstag in Berlin. Thousands of people gathered to see the spectacle.

☆ PEOPLE ARE OUTRAGED

Equivalent VIII (pictured on page 4 of this book) was created by the American sculptor **CARL ANDRE** in 1976. It is made up of a rectangle of bricks. When it was first displayed in London at the Tate Gallery, many people went to see it. Some were angry that the work was considered to be art.

☆ PEOPLE ARE INTRIGUED

The French artist **YVES KLEIN** held an exhibition called *Le Vide* in Paris in 1958. It consisted of a bare art gallery painted white inside and blue outside. It attracted many people.

50 What is the future of art?

Art will always be inspired by personal emotions and opinions, by world events and new technology.

Connections!

◉ The future of art depends on the future of life on Earth and how artists react to that.

"Art is an adventure into an unknown world which can be explored only by those willing to take risks."

QUOTE EXTRACTED FROM A LETTER SENT TO THE NEW YORK TIMES BY THE ABSTRACT EXPRESSIONISTS IN 1943.

☆ AN ARTIST MAY WORK TOGETHER WITH PEOPLE WHO DO NOT THINK OF THEMSELVES AS PROFESSIONAL ARTISTS. THEY MAY MAKE A WORK OF ART FOR THE COMMUNITY, SUCH AS A MURAL.

Connections!
ART
Index

abstract art 9, 10, 22
Abstract Expressionism 13, 15
academies 12
acid rain 21
acrylics 14
Africa 6, 10, 29
After the Bath, Woman Drying Herself 22
American Indians 6
ancient Egypt 7, 18, 19, 30
Andre, Carl 5, 13, 18, 31
animals 7, 10, 20
archaeology 18, 28
Arnolfini Wedding, The 15
Arp, Jean (Hans) 30
At the Moulin Rouge 29
automatism 30
avant-garde art 13
Aztec 28

Bacchus and Ariadne 12
Baroque 13
bas-relief sculpture 6
Bathers at La Grenouillère 13
Bathing Place, Asnières, A 18
Bayeux Tapestry 18
Beach at Trouville, The 5
beliefs 4, 6, 9, 12, 20
blindness 8
Boating on the Seine 16
bodies 15, 22
body painting 6, 10
bone 5, 6, 10
Book of Kells, The 19
Bosch, Hieronymus 24
Braille 8
Braque, Georges 10, 13
brushes 5, 15
Buddhism 27
Buncho 29
Byzantine art 19

calligraphy 4
cave paintings 5, 7, 10, 22
ceilings 7, 19
Cezanne, Paul 13
children's art 22, 28
China 10, 17, 25, 28
Christ Before the High Priest 27
Christo 31
churches 7, 24, 27
climate 21
Clock 9

collage 10, 12, 30
color 5, 8, 9, 12, 13,
    14, 16, 18, 19, 21, 29, 30
complementary color 16
conceptual art 9
conservation 30
Construccion 25
Constructivism 13, 30
Constable, John 13, 21
Crazy Horse 6
critics 13
Cubism 13

Dadaism 29
Dali, Salvador 13, 30
Da Vinci, Leonardo 10, 22, 31
Degas, Hilaire Germain Edgar 22, 29
De Kooning, Willem 15
Delacroix, Eugène 26
Derain, André 13
Di Bondone, Giotto 27
Disintegration of the Persistence of Memory, The 30
dreams 13, 22, 30
Duchamp, Marcel 29
Dürer, Albrecht 28

early art 5, 7, 10, 20, 21, 22, 25
easel picture 7
egg tempera 15
encaustic 14
Epstein, Jacob 9
Equivalent VIII 4, 31
Ernst, Max 13
exploration 28
Expressionism 13

Faa Iheihe 25
fame 10, 28, 31
Fauvism 13
feathers 5, 6, 19
feelings 9, 12, 13, 15, 16, 21, 24, 25, 29, 31
Fighting Téméraire, The 21, 30
floors 18
flowers 7, 8
forgery 31
Forrester, Sarah 25
Fountain 29
fractals 9
frame 7
freestanding sculpture 6

French Revolution 26
fresco 18, 21, 24, 27
function of art 6, 12
Futurism 9, 13

Gabo, Naum 13
Gauguin, Paul 25, 29
Gallaccio, Anya 7
galleries 7, 8, 21, 31
Garden of Earthly Delights 24
Gertler, Mark 8
Giacometti, Alberto 6
Gilbert & George 10
Goldsworthy, Andy 21
Gormley, Antony 22
gouache 14
Guernica 26

Hamilton, Richard 26
Hay Wain, The 21
Head Over Heels 7
hieroglyphs 7
Hinduism 27
Hirst, Damien 20
history 6
Hogarth, William 7

illuminated manuscripts 19
Impression, Sunrise 13
Impressionism 13, 14, 18, 22
Improvisations 22
Inca 28
Inuit art 17
Islamic art 4, 27

Japan 28, 29

Kahlo, Frida 25
Kandinsky, Wassily 22
Kirchner, Ernst 13
Klee, Paul 22
Klein, Yves 31
Kline, Franz 13
Kokoschka, Oskar 13
Kosuth, Joseph 9
Krishna and the Maidens 25

labeling art 13
landscape 7, 9, 14, 17, 21
Large Head of Diego 6
Last Supper, The 28
Les Demoiselles d'Avignon 29
Lewis, Wyndham 9

Liberty Leading the People 26
Lichtenstein, Roy 13, 26
light 7, 8, 13, 15, 16, 17, 21
Long, Richard 21

machinery 9, 13
Makin, Richard 19
manuscripts 19
Maoris 10
marble 7
Marilyn 25
Marinetti, Filippo Tommaso 13
Marriage Contract, The 7
masks 4, 6, 26, 29
Masks 29
materials 5, 6, 8, 10, 12, 17, 21, 32
Matisse, Henri 13
Merry-Go-Round 8
metal 4, 6, 7, 8, 13
Michelangelo 13, 19, 24, 27
Middle Ages 19
Milbanke and Melbourne Families, The 20
Millais, Sir John Everett 22
Minimalism 13
models 21, 24
Mona Lisa 10, 31
Monet, Claude 5, 13, 14, 17, 29
money 31
'Monument' for V. Tatlin 30
mosaic 18, 28
mosque 4
Mother and Child Divided 20
Munch, Edvard 25
mural 18
museums 7, 10, 22

naïve art 5
nature 20, 21, 22
Nigredo 19
1953 9
Nolde, Emil 29
Number 14 15

oil painting 14, 15
Oldenburg, Claes 26
144 Magnesium Square 18
Ophelia 22

Paik, Nam June 30
paint 6, 12, 14, 15
painting 4, 8, 9, 14, 15, 19, 20, 21, 22, 24

palace 7, 21, 24
palette 14, 15
papiers collés 10
papyrus 19
patrons 24
Pentecost, The 27
performance art 10
perspective 7, 27, 29
photography 9, 10, 12, 21, 28, 30
Picasso, Pablo 5, 7, 10, 13, 25, 26, 29, 31
pigment 14, 30
pointillism 18
Pollock, Jackson 13, 15
Polo, Marco 28
Pompeii 18, 28
pop art 13, 25, 26
Portrait of Matisse 13
pottery 4, 21, 27, 28
Pre-Raphaelite Brotherhood 22
"primitive" art 22
primary color 16
printing 28

Raphael 24
Real Work of Art, A 20
religion 10, 19, 24, 27
Renaissance 12, 13
Renoir, Pierre Auguste 13, 16
Romans 7, 12, 13, 18, 19, 27, 28
Romanticism 13
Rock Drill, The 9
Rousseau, Henri 5
rules 12, 22, 29

Scream, The 25
sculpture 4, 5, 6, 7, 8, 9, 10, 12, 13, 18, 20, 21, 22, 24, 26, 28, 29, 30, 31
secondary color 16
self-portrait 25
self-taught artists 5
senses 8
Seurat, Georges 18
Severini, Gino 13
shocking art 24, 29, 31
Sistine Chapel 19, 24
Slate Circle 21
Smith, W. Eugene 26
soil 5, 14
sound 8
Source of Scaur 21
Spanking New Brunette 25

spontaneous art 13, 30
stained glass 19
Stella, Frank 13
Still, Clyfford 9
stone 6, 7, 8, 14, 15, 17, 18, 21, 25, 28
Stonehenge 21
Stubbs, George 20
style 12, 13, 22, 25, 28
Sunflowers 16
Surrealism 13, 30

Talbot, William Henry Fox 10
Tatlin, Vladimir 13, 30
tattoo 4, 10
technology 28, 30, 31
television 28, 30
thermoform 8
Titian 12
totem poles 6
Toulouse-Lautrec, Henri 29
trompe-l'oeil 18
Turner, Joseph 13, 21, 30

ukiyo-e prints 29
Untitled (For Francis) 22

Van Eyck, Jan 15
Van Gogh, Vincent 14, 16, 29, 31
Van Gogh's Chair 14
Van Honthorst, Gerrit 27
Van Rijn, Rembrandt 17
Vauxcelles, Louis 13
Velazquez, Diego 13
virtual art 9
Vorticism 9

Wallinger, Mark 20
walls 7, 18, 28
war 6, 26
Warhol, Andy 13, 25
water colors 14
Water Lily Pond, The 17
weathering 21
Whaam! 26
Woman Bathing in a Stream 17
Woman in a Multicolored Hat 25
women in art 25
wood 5, 6, 12
world art 22, 28

☆ ACKNOWLEDGEMENTS Front cover: Ancient Art & Architecture: tr, cr, bl, bc ©ARS, NY & DACS, London 1996/Bridgeman: tl. Mary Evans/Explorer: tc. ©Succession Picasso/DACS 1996/National Gallery: br. Chris Taylor: cl. Back Cover: ©Richard Makin: tl. National Gallery/Bridgeman: cr. Gregory Sams/Science Photo Library: cl. Tony Stone: tr. P1 ©Caroline Grimshaw. P3 Ancient Art & Architecture: cr. P4 Ancient Art & Architecture: tr. ©Carl Andre/DACS, London/VAGA, New York 1996/Frank Hermann/Times Newspapers Ltd: c. Robert Harding: cl. P5 Ancient Art & Architecture: tr. ©DACS 1996/National Gallery/Visual Arts: bl. P6 ©ADAGP, Paris & DACS, London 1996/Bridgeman: tr. Ancient Art & Architecture: tl, tc, bl. Werner Forman Archive/University of British Columbia: br. P7 Ancient Art & Architecture: bl, bc. ©Anya Gallaccio/Courtesy Stephen Friedman Gallery, London: br. National Gallery/Bridgeman: c. P8 Tate Gallery/Bridgeman: c. P9 Tate Gallery: tr. Gregory Sams/Science Photo Library: br. P10 Jack Fields/Zefa: tl. Rex Features: bc, br. Tony Stone: bl. P11 ©Caroline Grimshaw: cl. National Gallery/Bridgeman: bc. P12 National Gallery: br. P13 ©ADAGP, Paris & DACS, London 1996/Philadelphia Museum of Art/Visual Arts: bc. ©DACS 1996/National Gallery/Bridgeman: bc. P14 Tate Gallery/Bridgeman: bc. P15 ©ARS, NY & DACS, London 1996/ Tate Gallery: bc. Camera Press Ltd: br. National Gallery/Bridgeman: tr. P16 National Gallery/Bridgeman: tr. National Gallery/Bridgeman: br. P17 ©DACS 1996/National Gallery/Bridgeman: tc. National Gallery/Bridgeman: tl. P18 AKG/Erich Lessing/Museo Nazionale Romano delle Terme, Rome: bl. ©Carl Andre/DACS, London/VAGA, New York 1996/Tate Gallery: br. National Gallery: cr. K.Scholz/Zefa: tl. P19 AKG/Erich Lessing: cr, bl. British Museum: tr. ©Richard Makin: br. Vatican Museums & Galleries/Bridgeman: tl. P20 British Museum: bl. Courtesy Jay Jopling, London: br. National Gallery/Bridgeman: bc. P21 ©Richard Long/Tate Gallery: cr. National Gallery/Bridgeman: c. Zefa: tr, br. P22 AKG/Erich Lessing: cl. ©Antony Gormley/Courtesy Jay Jopling/Tate Gallery: c. National Gallery/Bridgeman: tr. P23 ©Caroline Grimshaw: cr. Robert Harding: bl. P24 AKG/St. Annen-Museum, Lubeck: cr, Museo del Prado, Madrid: br. Vatican Museums & Galleries/Bridgeman: tr. Zefa: c. P25 ©ARS, NY & DACS, London 1996/Tate Gallery/Bridgeman: br. Mary Evans/Explorer: cl. ©Sarah Forrester: cr. ©La Licenciada Norma Rojas, Mexico/Bridgeman: tr. ©The Munch Museum/ The Munch-Ellingsen Group/DACS 1996/Nasjonal Galleriet, Oslo/Bridgeman: bl. ©Succession Picasso/DACS 1996/National Gallery: tc. Tate Gallery: bc. P26 Giraudon/Louvre, Paris/Bridgeman: tr. ©Roy Lichtenstein/DACS 1996/Tate Gallery/Bridgeman: b. ©Succession Picasso/DACS 1996/Prado, Madrid/Bridgeman: tl. P27 British Museum: br. National Gallery: tr. Bridgeman Art Library: tl. Victoria & Albert Museum/Bridgeman: bc, Michael Holford: cl. P28 Cleveland Museum of Art/Visual Arts: cr. P29 ©ADAGP, Paris & DACS, London 1996/Sidney Janis Gallery, New York/Rex Features: b. Bridgeman Art Library: c. British Museum/Bridgeman: tc. Christie's/Bridgeman: bc. ©The Nolde Foundation, Seebull/Nelson-Atkins Museum of Art, Kansas City: cl. ©Succession Picasso/DACS 1996/Museum of Modern Art, New York/AKG: tr. P30 ©ARS, NY & DACS, London 1996/Tate Gallery: bc. ©DERMAT PRO ARTE BV/DACS 1996/Bridgeman: tl. Frank Spooner: cr. Rex Features: br. P31 T. Sanpher: bl. EVERY EFFORT HAS BEEN MADE TO ACKNOWLEDGE CORRECTLY AND CONTACT THE SOURCE AND/OR COPYRIGHT HOLDER OF EACH PICTURE AND TWO-CAN PUBLISHING APOLOGISES FOR ANY UNINTENTIONAL ERRORS OR OMISSIONS WHICH WILL BE CORRECTED IN FUTURE EDITIONS OF THIS BOOK.